未来地球计划战略研究议程 2014

全球可持续发展研究战略优先领域

Strategic Research Agenda 2014

Priorities for a global sustainability research strategy

国际科学理事会未来地球计划临时秘书处　著
Future Earth Interim Secretariat, International Council for Science

王传艺　林　征　译
Translated by WANG Chuanyi and LIN Zheng

周天军　黄　磊　审校
Copyedited by ZHOU Tianjun and HUANG Lei

未来地球计划中国国家委员会秘书处
The Chinese National Committee for Future Earth Secretariat
中国科学院大气物理研究所大气科学和地球流体力学
数值模拟国家重点实验室　组织翻译
The State Key Laboratory of Numerical Modeling for
Atmospheric Sciences and Geophysical Fluid Dynamics,
Institute of Atmospheric Physics,
Chinese Academy of Sciences

气象出版社
China Meteorological Press

内容简介
Abstract

未来地球计划是由国际科学理事会、国际社会科学理事会、联合国教科文组织等多家国际科技组织联合发起的一项为期十年的大型科学计划。计划三大主题为：动态地球、全球发展和向可持续性转型，旨在应对全球环境变化挑战，通过科学家、决策者、科研资助机构、用户等相关利益团体之间协同设计、协同实施和协同产出，为国际社会提供面对全球环境变化挑战以及向可持续发展转型的跨学科集成研究。

经过未来地球计划科学委员会、参与委员会协同全球环境变化研究团体和来自商界、政府、民间团体等多方面社会利益相关者的多轮咨商和开放的网上调查，于2014年12月正式发布《未来地球计划战略研究议程2014》。该书结合三大研究主题细化了未来3～5年全球可持续发展研究的优先领域，是未来10年为促进全球可持续发展工作的纲领性文件，可供国内从事全球变化与可持续发展等相关研究、项目评议和资助的研究者、科技管理人员参阅。

图书在版编目(CIP)数据

未来地球计划战略研究议程2014：全球可持续发展研究战略优先领域：汉文，英文/国际科学理事会未来计划临时秘书处著；王传艺，林征译. —北京：气象出版社，2015.10

ISBN 978-7-5029-6272-2

Ⅰ. ①未… Ⅱ. ①国… ②王… ③林… Ⅲ. ①世界经济－经济可持续发展－研究－汉、英 Ⅳ. ①F11

中国版本图书馆CIP数据核字(2015)第239827号

未来地球计划战略研究议程2014　全球可持续发展研究战略优先领域

国际科学理事会未来地球计划临时秘书处 著　　王传艺 林 征 译

出版发行：气象出版社	
地　　址：北京市海淀区中关村南大街46号	**邮政编码**：100081
总 编 室：010-68407112	**发 行 部**：010-68409198
网　　址：http://www.qxcbs.com	**E-mail**：qxcbs@cma.gov.cn
责任编辑：李太宇	**终　　审**：贾鹏群
封面设计：易普锐创意	**责任技编**：赵相宁
印　　刷：北京地大天成印务有限公司	**印　　张**：6
开　　本：787 mm×1092 mm　1/16	**字　　数**：150千字
版　　次：2015年11月第一版	**印　　次**：2015年11月第一次印刷
定　　价：50.00元	

序　　言

全球环境变化问题是当代世界性重大课题。自20世纪中期以来，随着世界经济和人口的迅速增长，人类社会面临着全球环境变化带来的严峻挑战。1950年全球城市人口仅有7亿多，到2014年已增加到了39亿，预计到2050年全球城市人口将再增加25亿人，全球将有四分之三左右的人口生活在城市里。人类经济社会的快速发展、人口的增加和城镇化进程带来资源消耗加剧、生态环境破坏、生物多样性减少等一系列全球环境问题，人类活动排放的温室气体也造成了全球气候系统的持续变暖。根据政府间气候变化专门委员会（IPCC）发布的第五次气候变化评估报告，1880—2012年全球地表平均温度大约上升了0.85℃，北半球1983—2012年这30年的平均温度可能是过去1400年中最暖的。

自20世纪70年代以来，随着全球气候变暖、生态环境破坏、生物多样性减少等全球环境问题的不断恶化，全球变化的科学研究逐步兴起。为了更好地应对全球环境变化给人类社会带来的挑战，2012年6月“里约+20峰会”上国际科学界正式发起了“未来地球计划”，目的是重组现有的国际科研项目与资助体制，对地球系统开展更为系统、全面和深入的观测与研究，为全球可持续发展提供必要的理论知识、研究手段和方法，填补全球变化在科学研究与社会实践之间的鸿沟，使科学家的研究成果能更好地为全球可持续发展服务。为了更好地指导研究工作的开展，未来地球计划于2013年下半年启动了《战略研究议程2014》的编制工作，经过一年多的多方咨询与讨论，2014年12月4日，未来地球计划正式公布了《战略研究议程2014》。

《战略研究议程2014》指出，目前全球可持续发展面临着来自八大领域的严峻挑战。这八大领域涉及对水、能源和食物的需求，实现社会经济系统的去碳化，保护陆地、淡水和海洋自然资源，建设健康发展的城市，促进农村未来的可持续发展，改善人类健康，鼓励可持续、公平的消费和生产模式，提高社会应对未来威胁的恢复力等方面。对应全球可持续发展领域面临的重大挑战，《战略研究议程 2014》将“未来地球计划”的动态地球、全球可持续发展、向可持续性发展转型三大研究主题细化为九个子研究方向，确定了全球变化与可持续发展的 62 个具体研究问题，供不同领域、学科和地区的研究机构和组织设立优先发展和资助领域时参考。

为了充分利用国际资源、协同国内各方面力量以推动未来地球计划在中国的组织实施，中国科学技术协会组建了未来地球计划中国委员会（CNC－FE），确认了我国可持续发展中亟需解决的重点领域，为推动我国生态文明建设、为亚洲甚至世界在可持续性发展过程中遇到的类似问题提供成功案例作出贡献。为更好地使国内学者全面了解未来地球计划，CNC－FE 取得了国际未来地球计划的授权，组织精干力量将《战略研究议程 2014》进行了翻译。未来地球计划秘书处邀请国际科学界两位知名专家对中文版译文进行了审校，气象出版社对本书的出版给予了有力支持，我们在此一并表示衷心感谢！

本书涉及全球变化与可持续发展的几十个具体领域，限于译者学识水平，中文版译文不足之处在所难免，我们期待着广大读者的批评与指正。

未来地球计划中国国家委员会主席
中国科学技术协会副主席
中国科学院院士
秦大河

2015 年 11 月

引　言

未来地球计划是为向可持续发展转型提供所需知识而设计的全球研究平台。

未来地球计划寻求建立并联系可持续发展的知识体系，以提高多样化背景下研究的影响力，探索新的发展路径，并寻求加快向可持续发展转型的新方法。

本文件确定了未来3～5年全球变化和可持续发展优先研究领域。这些领域是经过全球学术界和社会团体广泛磋商的结果，意在提供解决方案导向型研究指导，以应对《未来地球计划2025年愿景》所提出的全球可持续发展重大挑战。

《战略研究议程2014》旨在为研究人员和资助者提供全球变化和可持续发展议程框架，确定未来3～5年重点优先研究领域，以便为制订研究战略和提供项目资助提供指南。

不同的领域、学科和地区的研究机构和利益相关者可参照《战略研究议程2014》设立优先发展和资助领域。未来地球计划每隔几年将发布新一版的战略研究议程。

以下八个图标代表了《未来地球计划2025年愿景》第一部分所阐述的全球可持续发展八大挑战。

Introduction

Future Earth is a global research platform designed to provide the knowledge needed to support transformations towards sustainability.

Future Earth seeks to build and connect knowledge to increase the impact of research in diverse contexts, to explore new development paths, and to find new ways to accelerate transitions to sustainable development.

This document identifies critical priorities for global change and sustainability research over the next 3 – 5 years. These priorities are the outcome of extensive discussion with scientists and societal partners globally, and are intended to provide guidance for solutions-oriented research to meet the global societal challenges identified in the *Future Earth* 2025 Vision.

The aims of the *Strategic Research Agenda* 2014 are to present a framework for global change and sustainability agenda setting for researchers and funders, and to identify key priorities for the next 3 – 5 years which can be used as starting points for the development of research strategies and funding programmes.

The Strategic Research Agenda 2014 is intended to be used across different domains, disciplines and regions of the world, by a range of different agencies and stakeholders, to inform priority-setting for research and research funding. A new Strategic Research Agenda will be developed and published by Future Earth every few years.

The icons represent the 8 global challenges described in part 1 of the Future Earth 2025 Vision.

关联

Nexus

去碳化

Decarbonisation

自然资产

Natural Capital

城市

Cities

农村未来发展

Rural Futures

健康

Health

消费

Consumption

治理

Governance

本书所用的八大挑战图标由 Curie Kure 所设计。
（http://curiekure.de/）.

The eight challenge icons used throughout were designed by Curie Kure
（http://curiekure.de/）.

目 录

Contents

未来地球计划 2025 年愿景

愿景

使人类生活在可持续发展、平等的世界里是未来地球计划的愿景。

科学需求

要实现这一愿景，需要一门能融合不同学科、不同知识体系和社会合作伙伴的**新型科学**，来支撑更灵活的全球创新体系。

任务

未来地球计划是专为向可持续发展转型提供知识而设计的**全球研究平台**。未来地球计划试图建立并联系可持续发展的**知识体系**，以提高研究在不同背景下的影响力，探索新的发展途径，并寻求**加速转型**的新方法。联合国可持续发展大会（Rio＋20）上提出，并在联合国大会支持下公布了全球可持续发展的目标，未来地球计划将有利于该目标的实现。

未来地球计划通过聚焦三个研究主题——**动态地球、全球可持续发展、向可持续性转型**，与社会团体一起共同开发能够支持各层面、各种条件下的决策者和社会转型所需的知识。

以下列出了未来地球计划为实现 2025 年愿景所需作出的贡献。

Future Earth 2025 Vision

Vision

The vision of Future Earth is for *people to thrive in a sustainable and equitable world*.

Science need

This requires contributions from a *new type of science* that links disciplines, knowledge systems and societal partners to support a more agile global innovation system.

Mission

Future Earth is a *global research platform* designed to provide the knowledge needed to support transformations towards sustainability. Future Earth seeks to build and connect *knowledge* to increase the impact of research in diverse contexts, to explore new development paths, and to find new ways to *accelerate transitions to sustainable development*. Future Earth will contribute to achieving goals on global sustainable development, as called for at the UN Conference on Sustainable Development (Rio+20) and subsequently articulated under the auspices of the UN General Assembly.

Future Earth will work with partners in society to co-develop the knowledge needed to support decision makers and societal change at all scales and in diverse contexts, by focusing on three Research Themes—*Dynamic planet*, *Global sustainable development* and *Transformations towards sustainability*.

The following outlines what Future Earth needs to have contributed to achieve its vision by 2025.

到 2025 年，未来地球计划将：

为什么需要
未来地球计划？

1　激励并创立与全球可持续发展重大挑战相关的突破性交叉科学

全球可持续发展关键挑战聚焦于：

（1）**满足全球对水、能源和食物的需求，建立水、能源与食物之间的协同和平衡管理**，理解这些相互作用如何受到环境、经济、社会和政治变化的影响。

（2）**实现社会经济系统去碳化以稳定气候**，促进技术、经济、社会、政治和行为向可持续性转型，为人类和生态系统构建有关气候变化影响和适应响应的知识体系。

（3）**保护支撑人类福祉的陆地、淡水和海洋自然资源**，了解生物多样性、生态系统功能和服务之间的关系，制定有效的评估和治理方法。

（4）**建设健康发展、恢复力强、生产力旺盛的城市**，探索既改善城镇环境和生活，又降低资源消耗的创新性实践，提供可以抵御灾害的高效服务与基础设施。

（5）**促进生物多样性、资源和气候变化的大背景下农村未来的可持续发展，以满足人类增长的需求**，研究土地利用、粮食系统和生态系统的不同发展途径，识别制度和治理需求。

By 2025 Future Earth will have:

WHY do we need Future Earth?

1 Inspired and created ground-breaking interdisciplinary science relevant to major global sustainability challenges

Key focal challenges are to:

(1) *Deliver water, energy, and food for all, and manage the synergies and trade-offs among them*, by understanding how these interactions are shaped by environmental, economic, social and political changes.

(2) *Decarbonise socio-economic systems to stabilise the climate* by promoting the technological, economic, social, political and behavioural changes enabling transformations, while building knowledge about the impacts of climate change and adaptation responses for people and ecosystems.

(3) *Safeguard the terrestrial, freshwater and marine natural assets underpinning human well-being* by understanding relationships between biodiversity, ecosystem functioning and services, and developing effective valuation and governance approaches.

(4) *Build healthy, resilient and productive cities* by identifying and shaping innovations that combine better urban environments and lives with declining resource footprints, and provide efficient services and infrastructures that are robust to disasters.

(5) *Promote sustainable rural futures to feed rising and more affluent populations* amidst changes in biodiversity, resources and climate by analysing alternative land uses, food systems and ecosystem options, and identifying institutional and governance needs.

（6）**改善人类健康**，阐明环境变化、污染、病原、疾病传播媒介、生态系统服务和人们生活、营养及福祉之间复杂的相互作用，找到应对措施。

（7）**鼓励可持续的、公平的消费和生产模式**，理解资源消耗的社会和环境影响，识别不依赖资源的增加人类福祉的机会，探索可持续发展之路及相关的人类行为转变。

（8）**提高社会应对未来威胁的恢复力，建立适应性治理系统**，形成全球联网风险阈值的早期预警，测试有效、可靠、透明的可持续性转型机制。

(6) *Improve human health* by elucidating, and finding responses to, the complex interactions amongst environmental change, pollution, pathogens, disease vectors, ecosystem services, and people's livelihoods, nutrition and well-being.

(7) *Encourage sustainable consumption and production patterns that are equitable* by understanding the social and environmental impacts of consumption of all resources, opportunities for decoupling resource use from growth in well-being, and options for sustainable development pathways and related changes in human behaviour.

(8) *Increase social resilience to future threats* by building adaptive governance systems, developing early warning of global and connected thresholds and risks, and testing effective, accountable and transparent institutions that promote transformations to sustainability.

未来地球计划产出什么成果?

2 提供社会团体应对全球可持续发展重大挑战所需的产品和服务

重点成果聚焦于:

(1)为及时观测和监测不同尺度上地球的状态、趋势和阈值(包括追踪指示性的快变过程和系统)提供**开放和包容的平台**。

(2)为评估人类福祉和可持续发展提供**具体指标和评估工具**。

(3)发展**新一代地球系统集成模式**,以增进对复杂的地球系统和人类活动动态的跨学科了解,为可持续发展决策提供系统的科学支撑。

(4)为提升人类经济社会包括降低风险灾害在内的恢复力提供**科学数据、工具和资源**。

(5)**为全球可持续发展提供转型途径的情景**,并评估不同转型策略和方案。

(6)为厘清全球可持续发展相关问题的争议提供重要的**科学评估和相关综合决策**。

(7)充分利用新科技、克服世界不同地区信息获取能力的差异,为全球变化和可持续性发展的**交流、参与和可视化提供创新性实践**。

WHAT will Future Earth deliver?

2 Delivered products and services that our societal partners need to meet these challenges

Key focal outputs are:

(1) *Open and inclusive platforms* for observing and monitoring the status, trends and thresholds of the planet in a timely manner at different scales, including tracking fast-changing sentinel processes and systems.

(2) *Tailored metrics and evaluation tools* for well-being and sustainable development.

(3) *New generation of integrated Earth system models* to deepen our understanding of complex Earth systems and human dynamics across different disciplines, and to underpin systems-based policies and strategies for sustainable development.

(4) *Science-based data, tool sand resources to support improved resilience* of people, communities and economies, including disaster risk reduction.

(5) *Scenarios for transformative development pathways that enable global sustainability*, to help evaluate different strategies and options.

(6) *Critical contributions to key debates on global sustainability issues*, including inputs to scientific assessments and decision-relevant syntheses.

(7) *Innovations in communicating, engaging and visualising global change and sustainability*, fully exploiting the potential of new technologies and overcoming differential access to information across the world.

未来地球计划如何开展？

3 运用前沿方法，协同设计并产出以解决问题为导向的全球可持续发展科学、知识体系和创新成果

重点研究方法聚焦于：

（1）开展能带动全世界**不同社会团体的**基础和应用研究，从而最大程度影响和响应社会需求，并且关注这些新方法的效用。

（2）将未来地球计划**打造为全球认可的、适用于全球各地区的可持续发展参与和协作研究模式**。

（3）**促进**讨论、示范优秀案例、动员一切力量进行**以解决问题为导向的全球可持续性发展科学、技术和创新**研发工作。

（4）**改变国际资助模式**，更好地支持跨地区和地区内的有利益相关者参与的交叉学科、跨学科研究。

（5）**促进**国家及国际研究机构和研究计划的**合作**，以便最大限度地利用可持续发展研究资源，扩大研究的影响力。

（6）促进**更先进的资料共享模式**，分享向可持续发展转变的环境变化和改进的数据，以支持不同层面的政策和实践。

HOW will Future Earth work?

3 Pioneered approaches to co-design and co-produce solutions-oriented science, knowledge and innovation for global sustainable development

Key approaches for focus are:

(1) Conducting fundamental and applied research in ways that *engage with diverse societal partners* across all regions of the world to maximise impact and responsiveness to society's needs, and monitoring the effectiveness of these new approaches to research.

(2) *Establishing Future Earth as a globally recognised model for engagement* and collaboration in research for global sustainable development, effective in all world regions.

(3) Stimulating debate, illustrating good practice and mobilising capacities for *solutions-oriented science, technology and innovation for sustainability*.

(4) *Changing international research funding practices* to better support interdisciplinary and transdisciplinary research and engagement across and within regions.

(5) *Fostering collaboration* among national and international agencies' research programmes, to maximise resources for and impacts of research towards sustainability.

(6) Contributing to *improved modes of sharing data* about environmental change and progress towards sustainability in order to support policy and practice at different levels.

未来地球计划要培养什么样的人才?

4 促进并动员跨越文化、社会、地域和年龄的力量，协同创造知识

重点领域聚焦于：

(1)激励和支持**新一代**能够进行全球可持续发展综合研究的**学者和实践者**，以传承未来地球计划的愿景和使命。

(2)打造由全世界各地区科学家、决策者、民间组织、企业家、资助者的**个人和组织**组成的**多元化又紧密联系的团体**。

(3)促使联合国系统、主要评估机构、可持续性发展目标制定者、代表性国家、主要产业、民间组织、城市网络等**具有重大影响力的全球利益相关者**的**参与**。

(4)**动员全世界各界的力量**，合作进行能够连接区域到全球过程的研究，提供可持续发展的多种路径选择。

(5)塑造一批坚信未来地球计划理念、并能担当未来地球计划大使角色的**核心科学家、决策者和民间组织领导人**，包括一批未来地球计划专家。

Who will Future Earth be?

4 Enabled and mobilised capacities to co-produce knowledge, across cultural and social differences, geographies and generations

Key areas for focus are:

(1) Inspiring and supporting *a new generation of scholars and practitioners* doing integrated science for global sustainability to carry forward Future Earth's vision and mission.

(2) Building a *diverse and connected community of participants and organisations*, including scientists, policy makers, civil society practitioners, private sector actors and funders from all regions of the world.

(3) *Engaging key influential stakeholders globally* in the UN system, major assessments, the sustainable development process, selected nations, and major industry, civil society and city networks.

(4) *Mobilising capacities in all parts of the world* to cooperate on research that connects local to global processes and promotes alternatives for sustainable development trajectories.

(5) *Creating a critical mass of scientists, policy makers and civil society leaders* who believe in and can serve as ambassadors for Future Earth, including a body of Future Earth Fellows.

战略研究议程 2014

全球可持续发展研究战略优先领域

与全球挑战密切相关的优先研究领域

下述优先研究领域按照《未来地球计划初步设计报告》所提出的概念框架组织，按照动态地球、全球可持续发展、可持续性转型三大主题分类。每一项优先研究领域均对应一个或多个《未来地球计划 2025 年愿景》所提出的全球可持续发展重大挑战。本书引言中给出了这些挑战的图标。

与社会协同产出知识

《战略研究议程 2014》所提出的不仅是一系列优先研究领域，它还倡导了一种新型的科研方式。这种方式在《未来地球计划 2025 愿景》中有详细阐述，它强调多学科的全面整合、吸纳社会合作伙伴参与协同设计和协同产出知识、强调国际合作、为决策者提供有价值的知识和提出社会所需的解决方案。

由研究人员和社会合作伙伴合作，协同设计并产出新知识，对发展科学的见解、数据和工具以应对最紧迫的全球可持续发展挑战至关重要。《战略研究议程 2014》呼吁研究人员和研究资助者与社会合作伙伴合作，制订研究重点并实施工作计划。这样科学才会在理解相关社会问题和提出解决方案方面发挥作用。

Strategic Research Agenda 2014

Priorities for a global sustainability research strategy

Research priorities linked to global challenges

The following research priorities are organised under the conceptual framework proposed in the Future Earth *Initial Design Report*. Research activities are grouped under the themes of Dynamic Planet, Global Sustainable Development, and Transformations towards Sustainability. Each priority addresses one or more of the critical global sustainability challenges set out in the Future Earth 2025 Vision. A key to the challenges is provided on the inner back cover.

Co-producing knowledge with society

The Strategic Research Agenda 2014 advocates not just a set of research priorities, but also a novel way of doing science. This approach is detailed in the *Future Earth* 2025 *Vision* and includes a strong emphasis on full integration among scientific disciplines, on engagement with societal partners in co-designing and co-producing knowledge, on international collaboration, on producing knowledge that is valuable to decision-makers, and on generating the solutions that society needs.

The co-design and co-production of new knowledge, created by researchers working in collaboration with their societal partners, is critical to developing scientific insights, data and tools that can contribute to addressing the most pressing global sustainability challenges. Across all the priorities presented here, researchers and research funders are urged to work with societal partners in developing and implementing their plans. In this way science will be contributing to understanding the problems that matter to society and developing the solutions that are needed.

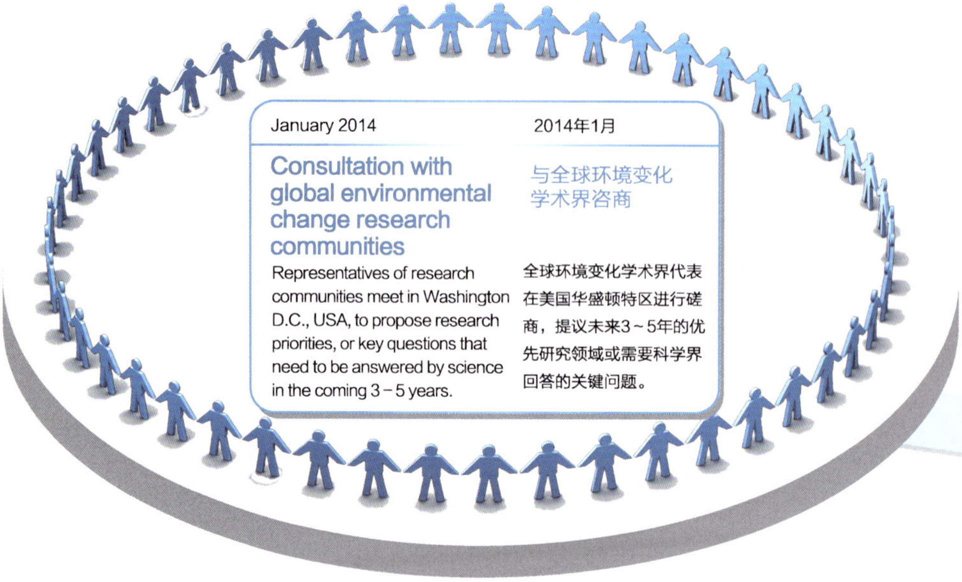

January 2014 2014年1月

Consultation with global environmental change research communities

与全球环境变化学术界咨商

Representatives of research communities meet in Washington D.C., USA, to propose research priorities, or key questions that need to be answered by science in the coming 3 – 5 years.

全球环境变化学术界代表在美国华盛顿特区进行磋商，提议未来3～5年的优先研究领域或需要科学界回答的关键问题。

450 research priorities

125 research priorities

May 2014 2014年5月

Priority setting workshop

设立优先研究领域研讨会

A multi-stakeholder workshop takes place in Kyoto, Japan, to review, discuss and prioritise the results.

多方面利益相关者研讨会在日本京都召开，对2014年1月会议结果进行审议、讨论并进行优先级排序。

June – August 2014 2014年6—8月

Final review

终审

The Future Earth Science Committee and interim Engagement Committee meet in Beijing, China, to review and refine the long list to a list of 62 research priorities, ready for publication.

未来地球计划科学委员会与过渡参与委员会在中国北京召开会议，进一步审议和精选优先研究领域名单，最终确定62项优先研究议题。

anuary – May 2014 2014年1—5月

esktop study 前期调研

n assessment of similar esearch priority-setting rocesses related to global hange and sustainable evelopment is undertaken.

对此前已有类似的全球变化和可持续发展优先研究领域的确立程序进行评估。

Co-design

The co-design of knowledge envisages that both researchers and societal partners are involved in defining research questions.

协同设计

研究人员和社会合作伙伴协同设计，共同参与优先研究问题的确定。

Collation of research priorities

优先研究领域整理

April – May 2014 2014年4—5月

Open online consultation 开放式网上咨询

An open online survey receives over 500 responses from people located in 74 countries worldwide. Survey respondents review and rank the priorities suggested so far, and suggest new priorities.

开放式的网上调查收到来自74个国家和地区的500余条回复。调查受访者对已有优先领域进行评议、排序并建议了新选项。

Origins and process

At the end of 2013, Future Earth was asked by one of its sponsors – the International Group of Funding Agencies for Global Change Research (IGFA)/Belmont Forum – to prepare a set of priorities for global sustainability research. The Strategic Research Agenda 2014 is a statement prepared by the Future Earth Science and Engagement Committees, on the basis of a process with three primary inputs: consultation with global environmental change research communities; engagement with societal partners; and assessment of the outputs of other recent priority setting processes relating to global change and sustainability research.

《战略研究议程2014》撰写起因及过程

2013年末，国际全球变化研究资助机构（IGFA）/贝尔蒙特论坛（未来地球计划资助机构之一）委托未来地球计划制订全球可持续发展的系列优先研究领域。应此要求，在与全球环境变化研究界协商、与社会合作伙伴合作并对近期全球变化和可持续发展优先级研究过程进行评估的基础上，未来地球计划科学委员会和参与委员共同完成了《战略研究议程2014》。

62 research priorities

战略研究议程 2014

A

动态地球

A1　观测并归因变化

A2　理解全球变化的过程、相互作用、风险和阈值

A3　探索并预测未来变化

B

全球可持续发展

B1　满足基本需求，消除不平等

B2　治理可持续性发展

B3　管理增长、协同和平衡

C

向可持续发展转型

C1　理解和评估转型

C2　确定和推广可持续发展行为

C3　转型发展路径

Strategic Research Agenda 2014

A

Dynamic Planet

A1 Observing and attributing change

A2 Understanding processes, interactions, risks and thresholds

A3 Exploring and predicting futures

B

Global Sustainable Development

B1 Meeting basic needs and overcoming inequalities

B2 Governing sustainable development

B3 Managing growth, synergies and trade-offs

C

Transformations towards Sustainability

C1 Understanding and evaluating transformations

C2 Identify and promoting sustainable behaviours

C3 Transforming development pathways

A

动态地球

本主题聚焦支撑全球和区域环境变化的物理、生态和社会机制方面的知识和证据，理解这些机制既往的相互作用和未来变化趋势。本部分的优先领域强调变化阈值、预警、学科综合以及新一代模式和数据需求。这些问题的提出旨在确定相关关键知识空白并利用现有知识，为应对全球可持续发展各项挑战，包括《联合国2015年后发展议程》和多元化的全球、区域和地方性的科学评估提供支撑。

A

Dynamic Planet

This theme focuses on knowledge and evidence about the physical, ecological and social mechanisms that underpin global and regional environmental changes, and understanding how these mechanisms have interacted in the past and are likely to change in the future. Our priorities here emphasize thresholds and early warnings, synthesis among disciplinary approaches, and new generations of models and their data needs. An effort is made to identify critical knowledge gaps and harness existing knowledge in support of challenges related to global sustainable development, including the United Nations (UN) post-2015 development agenda and scientific assessments relevant to diverse global, regional and local contexts.

A1

观测并归因变化

（1）地球系统（含地球生态系统和社会）过去如何变化？这些变化对响应当前环境变化有那些启示？区域及全球环境和社会变化的主要形态有哪些？从古生物学、考古学、人类学和历史学维度能获得哪些响应全球变化的新视角？

（2）不同区域和部门的大气污染物和温室气体排放怎样变化？碳和营养物质平衡怎样受其影响？社会驱动因素（如人口、财富、社会与技术变化、发展）起何作用？物理驱动因子（如大气传输和沉降、气候变化）起何作用？

（3）需要哪些模式来整合全球环境、社会一经济数据以支持全球（特别是欠发达国家）可持续发展？怎样发展并运用关联气候、健康、经济、制度变化数据和全球环境影响信息的方法来识别并监测可持续发展的关键领域和发展机遇？

A1

Observing and attributing change

(1) How has the Earth system, with its ecosystems and societies, changed in the past, and what can this tell us about current responses to environmental change? What are the main patterns in regional and global environmental and social changes? What new perspectives can be obtained by including paleontological, archaeological, anthropological and historical dimensions of responses?

(2) How are atmospheric emissions of pollutants and greenhouse gases changing in different regions and sectors, and how are carbon and nutrient balances affected? What is the contribution of social drivers such as population, wealth, social and technical change, and development? What is the contribution of physical drivers such as atmospheric transport and deposition, and changes in climate?

(3) What models do we need to integrate global environmental and socio-economic data to support progress towards global sustainable development, particularly in less developed countries? How do we develop and implement methods that link data on climate, health, economic and institutional change with information on impacts to identify and monitor key areas of concern and opportunities for development?

(4) 生物多样性、生态系统及其服务在不同空间尺度的历史、现状和未来发展趋势如何？哪些种类的生物多样性、生态系统及服务表现出最重要的发展趋势？这些趋势与人类福祉有哪些联系？

(5) 三个关键主题领域(土地利用变化、景观城镇化和城镇可持续发展)有哪些变化趋势？这三个领域的新一代监测系统(含可明确为相关决策所用的标准和指标)是怎样的？

(6) 如何建立一套全球变化的早期指标(特别是某些热点地区如三角洲、冰冻圈、山区、半干旱地区和热带雨林)？关键系统和热点地区的全球观测有哪些要求？怎样建立一个包括阈值和临界点的、综合的全球可持续发展评估体系？

(7) 需要哪些新的方法和技术，公开并透明地获取、组织、整合并提炼不同形式的大型、跨学科的知识和数据集(包括自然和工程科学、社会科学、自主和实践型基础知识)？怎样利用这些知识，支持并促进政府间气候变化专门委员会(IPCC)、生物多样性与生态系统服务政府间平台(IPBES)等科学评估？

(4) What are the historic and current status and trends of biodiversity, ecosystems and their services at different spatial scales? What kinds of biodiversity, ecosystems, services and places exhibit the most critical trends? What are the links between human well-being and these trends?

(5) What are the trends in three key topical areas of change—land-use change, landscape urbanisation and urban sustainability? What is the next generation of monitoring systems for these, including metrics and indicators that are demonstrably useful for informing decision-making?

(6) How should a suite of early indicators of critical global change be established, particularly in hotspot regions (e. g. deltas, cryosphere, mountain regions, semi-arid zones and tropical rainforests)? What are the requirements for global observatories of critical systems and hotspots? How should this effort support the creation of an integrated global sustainability assessment, including thresholds and tipping points?

(7) What new methods and technologies are needed to access, organise, integrate and summarise, in an open and transparent way, the large, interdisciplinary datasets covering different forms of knowledge and data, including natural and engineering science, social science, indigenous and practice-based knowledge? How can these be used to support and facilitate scientific assessments, such as IPCC and IPBES?

A2

理解全球变化的过程、相互作用、风险和阈值

(1) 受全球变化影响,全球粮食、城镇和金融体系在时间和空间上会发生怎样的相互作用和级联效应(反馈、远程耦合和系统性风险)?

(2) 大气成分的变化怎样影响生态系统的结构和功能?大气成分的变化怎样影响气候变化,尤其是极端事件的分布、强度、频率和降水形态?大气成分的变化怎样影响空气质量、碳平衡和不同生态系统的养分流动?怎样控制和调节这些影响?

(3) 不同尺度的生物多样性怎样影响其他全球环境变化?生物多样性在什么水平、何种程度上影响社会生态系统对全球环境变化的恢复力和适应力?全球尺度上保护或恢复生物多样性需要做到何种程度?

A2

Understanding processes, interactions, risks and thresholds

(1) What spatial and temporal interactions and cascading effects (feedbacks, tele-coupled and systemic risks) occur across global food, urban and financial systems as a consequence of global change?

(2) How do changes in atmospheric composition affect ecosystem structure and functioning? How do changes in atmospheric composition affect climate change, especially the distribution, intensity and frequency of extreme events, and precipitation patterns? How do changes in atmospheric composition affect air quality, carbon balances and nutrient flows in different ecosystems? How can these impacts be controlled and regulated?

(3) What is the role of biodiversity at multiple scales in affecting other global environmental changes? At what levels, and to what extent, does biodiversity contribute to the resilience and adaptability of socio-ecological systems to global environmental change? What level of protection or restoration of biodiversity is needed globally?

(4) 不同的演化过程，尤其是人类对不同物种直接或间接的选择，如何受全球环境变化的影响？这些演化过程如何通过粮食安全、生物入侵、抗生素和杀虫剂耐药性和污染等的反馈影响人类健康？

(5) 哪些关键水平的生物多样性变化影响生态系统产品和服务？哪些地方可以发现这些变化？生物多样性、生态系统及其服务过去和现在变化的主要驱动因素是什么？这些因素相互作用是叠加还是非叠加的？各种空间范围的生物多样性有何外在价值和内在价值？

(6) 未来不同尺度生态系统服务创造和维持过程中，生物物理、生态、经济和社会因素怎样相互作用？

(7) 沿海地区人类对灾害和环境退化脆弱性的主要驱动因素是什么？哪些因素有助于培养沿海城市和其他关键地区，特别是三角洲、河口、滨海湿地、岛屿、北极和珊瑚礁的恢复性发展？

(4) How are evolutionary processes—in particular the selection of different kinds of organisms directly or indirectly by humans-influenced by global environmental change? What are the feedbacks to human well-being, for example, through effects on food security, biological invasions, resistance to antibiotics and pesticides, and pollution?

(5) What are the critical levels of biodiversity change that impact ecosystem goods and services, and where can they be found? What are the main drivers (past and present) of change in biodiversity, ecosystems and their services, and do they interact additively or non-additively? What are the instrumental and non-instrumental values of biodiversity at a range of spatial scales?

(6) How will biophysical, ecological, economic and social factors interact in the future in creating and maintaining ecosystem services at different scales?

(7) What are the main drivers of human vulnerability to hazards and environmental degradation in coastal areas, and what factors foster resilient approaches to development in coastal cities and other critical zones, particularly deltas, estuaries, coastal wetlands, islands, the Arctic, and coral reefs?

(8) 超大城市和农村跨地域城镇化进程有哪些形态和驱动因素？何种程度上两者在全球范围内表现一致并相互关联？如何整合有关知识，促进可持续性定居决策？为实现向可持续性转型，城镇系统内部的相互作用、利益平衡和翻转点是怎样的？

(9) 生态系统服务变化和气候变化（包括疾病媒介、水源性疾病和人畜共患病的变化等）怎样影响人类健康？从局地到全球尺度上，哪些因素能调解与环境有关的健康影响？

(10) 社会、生态和气候系统存在哪些关键阈值和临界点？它们在多大程度上可预测？它们之间有哪些关联？哪些因素影响阈值检测和量化的程度？

(8) What are the patterns and drivers of urbanisation，ranging from megacities to rural settlements across geographical regions? To what extent are they globally consistent and connected? How can integrated knowledge help inform decisions about sustainable human settlement? What are the interactions，trade-offs and tipping points towards sustainability in urban systems?

(9) How is health influenced by changes in ecosystem services and climate，including changing disease vectors，water-borne diseases and zoonoses? What factors mediate the diffusion of environmentally-related health impacts from local to global levels?

(10) What are the thresholds and tipping points in critical social，ecological and climatic systems? How predictable are they，and what are the linkages between them? What influences the degree to which thresholds can be detected and quantified?

A3

探索并预测未来变化

(1) 怎样完善当前地球系统模式以更好地捕捉人类—环境相互作用的动力学机制，以支持风险预测以及年代际和更长的时间尺度上的适应？优先领域包括：改进气溶胶、云和污染物的耦合和反馈模式；提高对降水分布和强度以及冰冻圈变化的模拟；提高区域降尺度和城镇系统的模拟；整合土地利用实践和各类生态系统服务。

(2) 气候变率(含极端事件) 未来怎样变化？这些变化将怎样影响脆弱地区和人类？季节到年代际尺度上的极端气候事件发生的频率和强度的可预报性怎样变化？社会怎样利用这些预测降低风险，为人类生活、基础设施和环境创造发展机会？

(3) 受不同内在基本和表象变化因素驱动，不同生物群落的生物多样性、生态系统及其服务和潜在的社会影响未来合理的变化情景是什么？

A3

Exploring and predicting futures

(1) How can current Earth system models be improved to better capture the dynamics of human-environment interactions and support predictions of risks and adaptation on decadal and longer timescales? Key priorities are: to improve the coupling and feedbacks among aerosols, clouds and pollutants; to improve simulations of the distribution and intensity of precipitation and cryosphere changes; to increase regional downscaling and modelling of urban-systems; and to integrate land-use practices and ecosystem services.

(2) How will climate variability, including extreme events, change in the future and how will these changes influence vulnerable regions and people? How predictable are changes in the frequency and intensity of extreme climate-related events at seasonal to decadal scales? How can society use such predictions to reduce risks and create development opportunities for people, infrastructure and environment?

(3) What are plausible future scenarios of change in biodiversity, ecosystems, their services and potential social implications in different biomes, resulting from different underlying and proximate drivers of change?

（4）需要什么样的预测模型以预估与全球环境变化相关的新型疾病和健康威胁的后果？这些模型怎样才能有助于评估不同疾病和威胁预防策略并管控它们在国家、区域和全球范围内的影响？

（5）需要什么新型的社会经济模型以预估各种可持续生产和消费情景，识别障碍和平衡利益，评估风险（系统性或非线性的，社会性的或环境性的）和相关干预措施？

（6）怎样将人类个体和集体行为的计算模式集成到全球环境变化的地球系统模式中？哪些方面需要结合神经科学、心理学、人类学、社会学和经济学扩充新内容？这些模式怎样改变我们对未来人类行为、风险和利益平衡的理解？

(4) What predictive models are needed to project the consequences of the emergence of new diseases and health threats linked to global environmental change? How can these-models help to assess alternative strategies to prevent the emergence of these diseases and threats or manage their impacts at national，regional and global levels?

(5) What new socio-economic models are needed to project alternative scenarios of sustainable production and consumption，identify obstacles and trade-offs，and assess risks—whether systemic or non-linear，and social or environmental and related interventions?

(6) How can computational models of human individual and collective behaviour be integrated into Earth system models of global environmental change? What new aspects need to be developed，combining neuroscience，psychology，anthropology，sociology and economics? How do such models alter our understanding of future behaviours，risks and trade-offs?

B

全球可持续发展

本主题聚焦应对具体的当前可持续发展大挑战所需关键知识的差距，包括满足基本需求，呼应《联合国 2015 年后发展议程》提出的可持续发展优先领域。这些优先领域强调整合、协同产生知识以考察全球变化对贫困人群的影响、人类福祉基本需求之间的关系、全球可持续生产和消费的增长策略、城镇化、以及全球可持续发展能力的治理。

B

Global Sustainable Development

This theme focuses on critical knowledge gaps in ways of managing specific sustainable development challenges today, including meeting basic needs, and responding to emerging priorities in the UN post-2015 development agenda. Among other issues, these priorities emphasize integrated, co-produced knowledge to examine the effects of global environmental change on poor people, the nexus among basic needs for human well-being, growth strategies in relation to sustainable production and consumption, urbanisation, and governance for global sustainability.

B1

满足基本需求，消除不平等

(1)世界不同地区获得水源的方式怎样影响健康、生计和经济活动？超大城市水安全的最大威胁是什么？这些威胁怎样影响不同社会群体？

(2)不同能源（包括生物燃料）和能源技术（与温室气体排放、水资源利用和污染、生态系统服务、人类健康、平等和福祉相关）的生命周期意义如何？怎样考虑到这些不同方面，对从全球到个体家庭层面的能源策略进行全面综合的评估？

(3)就定居模式、基础设施、服务配置、空气和水质、废物处理和治理、经济增长、城镇生活方式和福祉方面而言，城市发展有哪些不同路径？这些路径怎样与风险、城市、区域和全球的可持续发展关联？

B1

Meeting basic needs and overcoming inequalities

(1) How does access to water affect health, livelihoods and economic activity in different regions of the world? What are the biggest threats to water security in megacities and how do they affect different social groups?

(2) What are the lifecycle implications of different energy sources, including biofuels, and energy technologies in terms of greenhouse gas emissions, water use and pollution, ecosystem services, and human health, equity and well-being? How can comprehensive, integrated energy assessments taking into account these different dimensions be developed from the global to the household scale?

(3) What are the different development pathways of cities, in terms of settlement patterns, infrastructure and service provisioning, air and water quality, waste management, governance, economic growth, urban lifestyles and well-being? How are these pathways related to risks, and to urban, regional and global sustainability?

(4)怎样保证地方、国家和全球的食品安全同时兼顾水、能源和其他生态系统,农业集约化对生态系统及其功能和人类福祉有什么影响?怎样平衡不同农业和渔业活动的生态系统服务和人类福祉之间的利益?

(5)不平等性怎样影响家庭、社区和国家实现可持续发展的能力?减缓和适应气候变化工作的变化怎样影响人类(特别是世界上最贫穷的人民)的脆弱性或福祉?

(6)不同经济增长战略对社会和经济成果(例如:贫困、不平等性、就业和生活质量)和环境(例如:气候稳定、生态系统健康和恢复力)有哪些影响后果?

(7)应采取哪些人类福祉和进步的措施和指标来支持《联合国2015年后发展议程》?监督和评估不同尺度的可持续发展目标需要哪些科学证据和分析?

(8)全球陆地和海上采掘业不断变化的结构、动态和前景如何?就环境和社会影响(包括提高效率和循环利用)而言,怎样更加可持续地利用不可再生资源?新兴的可持续和可再生能源业务动态如何?其对全球可持续发展有何贡献?

(4) How can local, national and global food security be met, taking account of water, energy and other ecosystem demands? What is the impact of agricultural intensification on ecosystems, ecosystem functions and human well-being? What are the trade-offs between different agricultural and fisheries practices for ecosystem services and human well-being?

(5) How does inequality influence household, community and state capacities to achieve sustainable development? How do changes in efforts to mitigate and adapt to climate change influence human vulnerability or well-being, particularly among the world's poorest peoples?

(6) What are the consequences of different economic growth strategies for social and economic outcomes (e.g. poverty, inequality, employment and quality of life) and for the environment (e.g. climate stabilisation, ecosystem health and resilence)?

(7) Which measures and metrics of human well-being and progress should support the UN post-2015 development agenda? What scientific evidence and analysis is needed to-monitor and evaluate sustainable development goals at different scales?

(8) What are the changing structures, dynamics and prospects for global extractive industries on land and at sea? How can non-renewable resource use be made more sustainable in terms of environmental and social impacts, including efficiency gains and recycling? What are the dynamics of emerging sustainable and renewable business-sectors? What is their contribution to global sustainability?

B2

治理可持续性发展

(1)全球性和区域性公共区域，如公海和极地地区面临哪些重大环境威胁？怎样加强管理这些区域的治理机制？

(2)需要哪些新的全球和政府间治理机制（包括金融手段）以确保人类发展和经济增长平等并充分考虑环境承受极限？

(3)从地方到全球范围的社会环境体系内在利益取舍的决策方法有哪些优势和缺点？其对生态系统服务的供应和监管有何影响？

(4)哪些机制可以最有效地提高政府和跨国金融机构透明度和责任制，促进可持续发展？如何实施并扩展？

B2

Governing sustainable development

(1) What are the major environmental threats in global and regional commons, such as the high seas and polar regions? How can governance mechanisms for managing these commons be strengthened?

(2) What new global and intergovernmental governance mechanisms, including financial instruments, are needed to ensure that human development and economic growth are equitable and respect environmental limits?

(3) What are the strengths and weaknesses of different decision-making approaches for balancing trade-offs inherent in socio-environmental systems from local to global scales? What are their impacts on the provision and regulation of ecosystem services?

(4) What are the most effective mechanisms for increasing the transparency and accountability of governments, multinational companies and financial institutions in order to promote sustainable development? How can these be implemented and scaled up?

(5)怎样完善机制设计，解决全球范围内市场和政策失误（例如：给生态系统服务或污染的社会成本定价）？其社会分配影响如何？

(6)地方团体和组织怎样参与全球环境变化活动？相关参与活动在减少环境影响，提高对全球变化的恢复力方面怎样做得更有效、更合法？

(7)哪些可持续发展战略在不同的公共和个人环境中起效？这些战略怎样相互影响？证据和分析，利益和联合在这些战略中发挥怎样的作用？

(5) How can mechanisms best be designed to address market and policy failures (e. g. by pricing ecosystem services or the social cost of pollution) that are effective and can also reach the global scale? What are their distributive social effects?

(6) How do local communities and organisations participate in global environmental change activities? How can participation be made more effective and legitimate in reducing impacts, and increasing resilience to global environmental change?

(7) What sustainable development strategies work in different public and private contexts? How do public and private sustainability strategies influence each other? What role do evidence and analysis, and interests and alliances, play in these strategies?

B3

管理增长、协同和平衡

(1)怎样通过生产和消费集成策略，显著增加水、能源和营养物的利用率，以满足不断增长的食品(来自陆地和海洋的)、水和能源需求？粮食生产、水资源和能源利用之间的协同和平衡机制有哪些？如何管理以确保人们公平地获取这些资源？

(2)怎样识别、测定、预测、避免或解决根据人口和环境变化预估的资源利用的潜在冲突？

(3)不同国家和行业能采用哪些脱碳能源系统路径？其中哪些具有经济、社会和环境可行性，怎样实现？能源和经济增长之间的平衡、协同和获取问题之间关系如何？

(4)(与不作为相比)减缓或适应气候变化等全球环境变化有哪些长期的经济、社会成本和收益？

B3

Managing growth, synergies and trade-offs

(1) How can the growing demand for food (terrestrial and marine), water and energy be met through integrated production and consumption strategies that significantly increase the efficiency of water, energy and nutrient use? What are the synergies and trade-offs between food production, water use and energy use? How can these be managed to secure equitable access?

(2) How can potential conflicts over resource use be identified, mapped, predicted, and avoided or resolved under projected demographic and environmental change?

(3) What pathways to decarbonised energy systems are available for different countries and business sectors? Which of these are economically, socially and environmentally feasible, and how can they be achieved? What are the trade-offs, synergies and issues of access in relation to energy and economic growth?

(4) What are the long-term economic and social costs and benefits of different approaches to mitigating or adapting to climate change and other global environmental changes (compared to inaction)?

(5)不同的生态系统服务之间有哪些协同和平衡机制？可开发哪些工具来有效评估不同空间尺度的平衡机制？在需要平衡取舍时，怎样确定首选解决方案？

(6)不同的土地利用变化对生物多样性、生态系统及其服务有何影响？

(7)城镇化怎样影响农村地区和不同规模的生态系统？城乡之间能量、物质和生态系统服务时空流动(供给和需求)如何？有哪些有效且公平的管理策略？

(8)人口变化对可持续发展和人类福祉有何影响？

(5) What are the synergies and trade-offs among different ecosystem services? What tools can be developed to assess these trade-offs robustly at a range of spatial scales, and how should preferred solutions be chosen when trade-offs exist?

(6) What are the implications of different land-use changes on biodiversity, ecosystems and their services?

(7) How does urbanisation impact rural communities and ecosystems across scales? What are the spatial and temporal flows (supply and demand) of energy, materials and eco-system services between urban and rural systems? What are effective and equitable management strategies?

(8) What are the implications of demographic changes for sustainable development and human well-being?

C

向可持续发展转型

本主题聚焦社会通过转型来应对全球环境及可持续发展挑战所需的关键知识欠缺。它将有助于识别社会文化、经济、体制和政治障碍和机遇，以及实现经济繁荣、社会公正、健康生物圈的可持续发展所需机制。本部分问题的提出在于观察和评估各种社会转型、转型过程中的内在利益平衡、冲突，以及不同情况下影响转型路径的因素。

C

Transformations towards Sustainability

This theme addresses critical knowledge gaps in how societies might address global environmental and sustainability challenges through transformative change. It helps to identify socio-cultural, economic, institutional and political barriers and opportunities, and the mechanisms needed to promote sustainable development pathways linking economic prosperity with social justice and a healthy biosphere. The questions posed here address observation and assessment of societal transformations, the trade-offs and conflicts inherent to transformation processes, and factors influencing transformation pathways in different contexts.

C1

理解和评估转型

(1)现有粮食、能源的生产以及消费模式和情景的基本假设(尤其是关于需求和分配、贫困、技术和行为)有哪些?不同意识形态和可持续发展形式怎样影响相关研究和社会/公共政策?对不同发展形式的理解怎样才能转化为可行的模式?

(2)新技术(如纳米技术、生物技术、生物工程和地球工程)伴随哪些机遇和风险?新技术的兴起涉及哪些利益平衡,带来哪些影响(包括环境变化背景下其社会分配效应)?怎样评估新技术、产品和服务对全球和地方可持续发展的影响?

(3)社会系统怎样启动转型?在社会生态和社会技术系统转型过程中,人类机构和集体行动怎样发挥作用?怎样观测和模拟复杂的社会生态系统转型变化?

C1

Understanding and evaluating transformations

(1) What are the underlying assumptions (particularly regarding demand and distribution, poverty, technology and behaviour) associated with existing models and scenarios of food and energy production and consumption? How do diverse ideologies and visions of development influence research programmes and social/public policies? How can an appreciation of diverse visions of sustainability translate into the identification of plausible alternative models for action?

(2) What opportunities and risks might arise from new technologies (e. g. nanotechnology, biotechnology, bioengineering and geoengineering)? What are the trade-offs and implications associated with new technologies, including their distributive social effects in the context of environmental change? How can the impacts of new technologies, products and services on global and local sustainability outcomes be assessed?

(3) How are transformations initiated in social systems? What is the role of human agency and collective action in influencing transitions in socio-ecological and socio-technological systems? How can transformative change in complex socio-ecological systems be observed and modelled?

(4)在某些地区(如:沿海地区、城市、低洼岛屿、山区残遗种保护区)达到适应极限时能采取哪些可能的"退出策略"?这些适应性限制对社会、政治、道德以及公正和公平的影响有哪些?

(5)社会对自然资源的管理怎样划分优先次序:(a)保护;(b)恢复已经退化或耗尽资源系统;或(c)提高系统的设计和效率,使利益最大化或减少影响?这些管理方法对实现不同范围和不同条件下自然资源可持续利用的转型有怎样的重要性?

(6)全球和地区不同的政治经济怎样影响不同领域的可持续发展转型?处理转型过程中依赖性问题和现行政治惯性有哪些管理方面的挑战?结构变化怎样激发权力不平等和不确定性条件下的可持续发展解决方案创新?

(4) What are possible 'withdrawal strategies' (e.g. for coastal communities, cities, lowlying islands, mountain refugia) when limits to adaptation are reached? What are the social, political and ethical implications of these limits, and what are the implications for justice and equity?

(5) How should society prioritise the management of natural resources: (a) conservation, (b) restoration of systems where resources have been degraded or exhausted, or (c) improving the design and efficiency of systems to maximise benefits or reduce impact? What is the relative importance of these management approaches at different scales and in different contexts for the transition towards sustainable use of natural resources?

(6) How do global and regional political economies influence transformations to sustainability in different domains? What are the governance challenges in dealing with path dependency and the inertia of incumbent regimes? How can structural changes motivate innovative sustainable solutions under conditions of power inequalities and uncertainty?

C2

确定和推广可持续发展行为

(1)怎样界定和测量不同社会和经济环境下的可持续性消费？社会和生态非可持续性消费实践和模式背后的驱动因素是什么？这些因素和实践如何向可持续发展转化？

(2)在全球环境变化的背景下人们的文化价值观、信仰、世界观和道德如何演变？这些因素如何影响和塑造与环境有关的个人和集体的态度和行为，包括生活方式的选择和做法？与可持续性相关的个人价值观和共同价值观之间有怎样的关系？

(3)不同社会经济和文化背景下的创新和可持续发展实践多大程度上可转化？个人、社区和公共部门的技术、社会、体制和文化方面的创新怎样塑造可持续发展的转变？加强创新体系以应对全球环境和社会变化需要什么样的激励机制和政治程序？

C2

Identifying and promoting sustainable behaviours

(1) How can sustainable consumption be defined and measured in different social and economic contexts? What are the drivers behind socially and ecologically unsustainable consumption practices and patterns? How can these drivers and practices be transformed?

(2) In what ways are cultural values, beliefs, world views and ethics evolving in the context of global environmental change? How do they influence and shape individual and collective attitudes and behaviour relating to the environment, including lifestyle choices, and practices? How do individual values relevant to sustainability relate to shared values?

(3) How transferable are innovative and sustainable practices in different socio-economic and cultural contexts? How does technological, social, institutional and cultural innovation in private, community and public sectors shape sustainability transitions? What incentives and political processes are needed to strengthen systems of innovation to respond to global environmental and social change?

(4) 不同社会和文化环境(包括不同城镇环境)下,人们对渐变和突发的环境变化和事件怎样感知并采取行动? 为响应全球环境变化而产生的新的学习形式和信息共享方式怎样演变? 这些怎样影响人们的看法、集体行动和政策响应?

(5)通信和网络技术怎样为信息交流、协作和为实现可持续发展的集体行动提供便利? 这些技术怎样促进不同群体的社会融合和参与应对气候变化?

(4) How are gradual and sudden environmental changes and events perceived and acted upon in different social and cultural contexts, including diverse urban environments? How are new forms of learning and information sharing evolving in response to global environmental change, and in what ways are these influencing perceptions, collective action and policy responses?

(5) How do communication and networking technologies facilitate information exchange, collaboration and collective action for promoting systemic change towards sustainability? In what ways can these technologies promote social inclusion and participation of diverse groups in societal responses to climate change?

C3

转型发展路径

(1)评估生物多样性和生态系统服务的各种新形式怎样在国家和区域层面上影响宏观经济政策？哪些方法有助于平衡生物多样性和生态系统服务的经济和非经济价值，并为生态系统管理战略的制定提供信息？

(2)在城镇和农村地区以及不同的社会经济环境中各系统有制约因素和相互依赖关系，调整和转化这些地区的基础设施和服务有哪些潜力和可能性？哪些类型的规划流程和工具有助于统筹城乡可持续发展？

(3)变化的社会经济条件(如收入和教育、保健资源的获取)怎样影响包括消费行为在内的对环境的态度和行动？经济繁荣和增长模式怎样影响社会可持续发展路径？使经济增长与环境退化解耦最有前途的政策方法有哪些？商业和市场的作用如何？

C3

Transforming development pathways

(1) How are new forms of valuing biodiversity and ecosystem services influencing macro economic policies at national and regional levels? What approaches can help balance the economic and non-economic values of biodiversity and ecosystem services, and inform the development of ecosystem management strategies?

(2) What are the potentials and possibilities for adapting and transforming infrastructure and services in urban and rural areas, in diverse socio-economic contexts, given the constraints and interdependence of these systems? What types of planning processes and tools can contribute to integrated urban and rural sustainable development?

(3) In what ways do changing socio-economic conditions, such as changes in income or access to education and health care, affect attitudes and actions towards the environment, including consumption practices? How can alternative models of prosperity and growth influence sustainability pathways? What are the most promising policy approaches to decoupling economic growth from environmental degradation? What is the role of business and the market?

(4)各类叙述方式(特别是关于发展、未来、正义、风险和灾难、冲突的叙述方式)在驱动人类行为和社会变化(包括决策)方面的性质和作用是什么?这些叙述方式可能会以何种方式影响风险减缓,激励可持续发展变革行动?

(5)哪些新的治理机制和方法有助于社会向可持续发展转型?不同机制安排的优势和局限有哪些?用于治理全球共性问题的机制与区域和地方层面的治理机制有什么差距和不匹配?在不同情境下如何评估和推进可持续转化的治理机制?

(4) What is the nature and role of narratives (particularly around development, futures, justice, risk and disasters, conflicts) in driving human behaviour and social change, including decision-making? In what ways might these narratives influence risk-mitigation and inspire transformative action towards sustainability?

(5) What novel types of institutions and approaches to governance can help societies transition to sustainability? What are the strengths and limitations of different institutional arrangements for these transitions? What are the gaps and mismatches between institutions designed to govern the global commons and those designed at the regional and local levels? How can different governance systems enabling transformations to sustainability be evaluated and promoted in different contexts?

附录1 未来地球计划科学委员会、参与委员会委员及执行主任简介

Appendix 1 Brief Introduction to Future Earth Science Committee, Engagement Committee Members and Executive Director

未来地球计划科学委员会由18位专家组成。

Mark Stafford Smith，主席

Mark Stafford Smith，澳大利亚联邦科学与工业研究组织（CSIRO）气候适应旗舰项目科学主任，负责指导气候变化适应领域内高度跨学科项目。他在旱地系统生态学、管理和决策方面有30余年工作经验，曾担任包括位于爱丽斯泉的CSIRO中心干旱区项目负责人和沙漠知识合作研究中心CEO等高级职务。在此期间，他领导了国际地圈生物圈计划（IGBP）全球变化与陆地生态系统核心项目，他也是AridNET国际网络重要完成人，设计了旱地发展范式。近年来研究重点逐渐转向气候变化适应。受国际科学理事会任命，担任IGBP科学委员会成员和副主席（2003—2009），并担任了“压力之下的地球：为全球环境变化提供新知识”国际会议联合主席，该会议为2012年联合国可持续发展里约热内卢大会奠定了基础。

Belinda Reyers，副主席

Belinda Reyers，南非科学和工业研究理事会（CSIR）首席科学家，领导生物多样性和生态系统服务研究小组，工作重点在生态系统服务，关注其条件、管理、与社会发展和消除贫困的联系，以及全球变化对这些关系的影响。她是南非斯泰伦博斯大学生态保护与昆虫学系副教授和瑞典斯德哥尔摩大学斯德哥尔摩恢复力中心的高级研究员、非洲保护生物学会理事会成员、生物多样性计划（DIVERSITAS）科学委员会成员和对地观测组织生物多样性观测网络

（GEOBON）生态系统服务组联合主席。她一直担任南非政府生物多样性和生态系统服务目标及指标顾问，为参加联合国生物多样性和生态系统服务政府间平台（IPBES）大会的南非首席谈判代表提供科学支持。

Melissa Leach，副主席

Melissa Leach，英国苏塞克斯大学发展研究所主任，2006—2014 年期间负责英国经济与社会研究理事会社会技术和环境可持续发展中心（www.steps-centre.org）。作为地理学家和社会人类学家，她在非洲和其他地区的研究整合了社会科学、科学与政策和自然科学，涵盖了环境、农业、卫生、技术和性别多个领域，并有大量论著出版，包括《误读非洲景观》（剑桥大学出版社，1996）、《重组森林砍伐》（Routledge 出版社，1998）、《科学，社会与能源》（剑桥大学出版社，2003 年）、《土地的谎言：挑战非洲环境常见观念》（James Currey 出版社，1996）、《动态的可持续性：科技、环境和社会公正》（Earthscan 出版社，2010 年）和《绿色拼抢》（Taylor and Francis 出版社，2012）。她曾领导并管理许多大型跨学科研究和政策参与计划，包括“创新、可持续性、发展：一个新宣言”（www.anewmanifesto.org，2010 年至今）和由生态系统服务扶贫计划（ESPA）资助的由 19 个合作方组成的非洲联盟疾病的动态驱动因素项目（2011—2015 年）。

Bina Agarwal

Bina Agarwal，英国曼彻斯特大学经济发展与环境教授、国际生态经济学协会主席。曾任印度德里经济增长研究所所长。早年就读于剑桥大学和德里大学，曾在哈佛大学、普林斯顿大学和明尼苏达大学工作。她是国际经济学联盟副主席以及国际女性主义经济学联盟主席、经济效益衡量委员会委员、生态系统变化与社会计划成员、联合国发展政策委员会成员、印度土地改革全国委员会成员。发表的论著涵盖环境、食品安全、土地与生活方式、性别、贫穷与社会不平等，包括：《自己的领地：南亚性别和土地权》（剑桥大学出版社，1994）和《性别与绿色治理》（牛津大学出版社，2010）。2008 年，获得印度总统颁发的 Padma Shri 奖。2010 年，因推动经济学前沿思想的贡献获得美国塔夫茨大学颁发的 Leontief 奖。

Xuemei Bai

白雪梅，澳大利亚国立大学芬纳环境和社会学院城市环境和人类生态学教授，研究重点是城市可持续发展科学，包括城市化与地方、区域和全球尺度环境变化、城市系统时空动态、城市与气候变化、城市政策与管理、城市化对农业生产和粮食安全的影响，以及中国环境政策等。她的研究重点在亚太区域。曾任国际全球环境变化人文因素计划(IHDP)副主席，IHDP 产业转型核心项目科学指导委员会委员。白教授是《千年生态系统评估以及全球能源评估》的主要作者，在中国、日本及美国国家科学院多个高级别政策研究委员会任职。

Eduardo S. Brondizio

Eduardo S. Brondizio，美国印第安纳大学伯明顿分校人类学教授(2005—2012 年任人类学系主任)，全球环境变化人类学培训研究中心、Vincent & Elinor Ostrom 政治理论及政策分析中心成员，目前任巴黎高级研究院研究员。他是 IGBP 科学委员会委员，IHDP 和 DIVERSITAS 的合作者。作为一位致力于亚马逊乡村人口跨学科研究的环境人类学家，Brondizio 教授的研究考察社会经济学、人口统计学以及公共政策和环境变化之间的相互作用。他在土地和农业、小农生活、环境变化与适应及与商品链的相互作用，以及乡村发展与贫穷方面有诸多论著发表。近期来着力研究多层次的社会经济、人口、体制和环境变化的相互作用。参与了千年生态系统评估、生态系统和生物多样性经济学计划以及 IPBES 工作。

Bradley Cardinale

Bradley Cardinale，淡水生态学家。他运用理论和实验以及数据分析方法研究和预测生物多样性消失对人类的影响，以及复原退化的生态系统所带来的冲击。其最著名的研究成果是基于元分析理论预测生物多样性对生态系统，以及该生态系统给人类提供商品和服务能力的影响。现为美国密歇根大学副教授，并任该校自然资源与环境学院生态保持计划主任。他于 2002 年在美国马里兰大学获博士学位，随后在威斯康星大学麦迪逊分校完成博士后研究。已发表了 70 多篇学术论文，获得过包括 Hynes Award 在内的多个奖项。目前担任Ecology and Ecological Monographs 杂志编辑，并当选 DIVERSITAS

淡水生物多样性委员会委员。

Sandra Díaz

Sandra Díaz,阿根廷科尔多瓦国立大学生态系统与生态学系教授,阿根廷国家研究理事会高级研究员,研究兴趣是植物功能性状及其与全球变化之间的相互作用。近年来,她以功能多样性如何影响生态系统的概念在社会发展中的应用方面的研究而著称。2009年当选美国国家科学院外籍院士,2010年当选发展中国家科学院院士和阿根廷科学院院士。曾于1998年获阿根廷植物学会奖,2002年获古根海姆奖学金,2008年获美国柯查莱利奖,2009年获美国生态学会可持续研究科学奖,2011年获巴西科学协会奖和加拿大政府奖。她参加了千年生态系统评估和IPCC工作。她是DIVERSITAS科学委员会委员,也是国际Núcleo DiverSus on生物多样性和可持续性计划的创始人和主任。

Armin Grunwald

Armin Grunwald,德国卡尔斯鲁厄理工学院技术哲学与伦理学教授,任该学院技术评估与系统研究所所长、德国国会技术评估办公室主任。Grunwald教授的主要研究领域包括技术评估方法学、可持续发展、以及新兴技术(如纳米技术)的技术伦理学。他是巴登符腾堡州可持续发展顾问委员会成员,也是州科学、研究和艺术部科学促进可持续发展专家组成员。

Heinz Gutscher

Heinz Gutscher,瑞士苏黎世大学社会心理学名誉教授,瑞士人文与社会科学学院院长、瑞士气候与全球变化论坛主席。自2013年起担任多物种论坛科学指导委员会委员,已从事与环境和可持续发展有关的社会心理学研究方面20余年。研究兴趣包括社会影响过程的形式功能和机制、信任与自信、可持续发展问题的社会心理学、风险洞察和风险的交流、变化管理、大规模社会干预/运动的规划和评估、社会心理学知识在能源、流动性、消费和新技术接受领域的应用。

Corinne Le Quéré

Corinne Le Quéré,英国东英吉利大学气候变化科学与政策教授、丁铎尔气候变化研究中心主任。研究重点是气候变化和碳循环(包括自然环境和社会)之间的相互作用。她发展了一种新的理论和观测相结合的模式,可以定量地衡量社会心理变化驱动的大气二氧化碳浓度的变化。Le Quéré 教授是 IPCC 第三、四和五次评估及千年生态系统评估的作者。她也是全球碳计划的共同主席,在每年发表的《全球碳预算》中发挥主导作用。Le Quéré 教授早年毕业于蒙特利尔大学物理学专业,在麦吉尔大学获大气和海洋科学硕士学位,1999 年在巴黎第六大学获海洋学博士学位,曾在美国普林斯顿大学、德国马普生物地球化学研究所和英国南极调查局从事研究工作。

Cheikh Mbow

Cheikh Mbow,世界农林业中心气候变化和发展研究中心(位于肯尼亚内罗毕)资深科学家,兼任美国密歇根州立大学农林系副教授。他是 IGBP 科学委员会委员(2012—2013)和 IPCC 第五次评估报告工作组主要作者(第 11 章:农业、林业和其他土地用途)。Cheikh Mbow 博士曾在南非谢赫安塔迪奥普大学环境科学学院任副教授,从事遥感—地理信息系统和气候变化研究 11 年。他是区域稀树草原植物系统扰动研究专家,对森林火灾和其他农村土地覆盖变化的影响研究有较深造诣,在地面碳储量评估、面向碳收支模型的植被调查以及植被群落监测方面研究经验丰富。

Susanne Moser

Susanne Moser,美国 Susanne Moser 研究与咨询公司的首席研究员、加州大学圣克鲁兹分校海洋科学研究所助理研究员、斯坦福大学森林环境研究所研究员。作为气候变化适应、社会变化交流及科学与政策互动领域国际知名学者,她与美国、欧洲和澳大利亚政府和非政府组织的研究学者有广泛合作。她于 1997 年在克拉克大学获地理学博士学位,具有很强的跨学科专长,曾在美国大气研究中心华盛顿亨氏中心和忧思科学家联盟工作。她曾在 IHDP 科学顾问委员会、美国国家研究委员会、美国国家气候评估中心等多个组织和机构任职。参与了 IPCC 第四次和第五次评估报告的编写,是 IPCC 极端事件与灾难管理和适应特别报告的编审。她是 Aldo Leopold 领导奖、Kavli 科学前沿奖、Donella Meadows 领导奖、Google 科学交流奖和 Walton 可持续方案项目的获得者。

Karen O'Brien

Karen O'Brien，挪威奥斯陆大学社会学和人类地理学系教授，主要研究气候变化及其影响、人类安全的脆弱性和适应性，以及全球环境变化和全球化之间的联系。目前主要关注社会化过程适应性问题以及未来气候变化情况下青年的愿景与价值观。O'Brien 教授对意识和合作能力在转型过程中的作用以及人、文化和各系统转型的联系有浓厚研究兴趣。她的研究强调跨学科综合研究的重要性。她曾参与了 IPCC 第四次和第五次评估报告以及风险促进气候变化适应特别报告（SREX）的撰写。

Dahe Qin

秦大河，冰川学家和气候学家，中国科学院院士、第三世界科学院院士，主要研究南极冰川和冰冻圈物理过程。他是气候和环境的古生物记录研究领域的专家，是中国科学院冰冻圈国家重点实验室的创建者。他曾任中国气象局局长，领导了《中国气象事业战略发展研究》。他也是第三次 IPCC 科学评估报告的主要作者，第四、第五次报告的共同主席。他是 IPCC 团队的主要参与者，该团队 2007 年获诺贝尔和平奖。曾荣获过多项奖项和嘉奖。因为他在科学研究中的杰出工作，获得国际气象组织奖。发表科学论著 300 余篇（部）。

Youba Sokona

Youba Sokona，可持续发展南方中心特别顾问。该中心是致力于分析发展中的问题和经验，为提供发展中国家在国际舞台上的集体和单个行动提供所需智力和政策支持的发展中国家政府间组织。他曾在联合国非洲经济委员会非洲气候政策中心（ACPC）任协调员，直至 2012 年 5 月。2004—2010 年，任撒哈拉和萨赫勒观测站（OSS）执行秘书。其研究重点是能源、环境和可持续发展之间的关系，在非洲方政策方面工作经验丰富。此前他曾在塞内加尔的第三世界环境发展协会工作，在马里巴马科高等工程学院任教授。他曾在多个非洲政府部门担任咨询顾问，已发表了多篇关于非洲能源、环境与发展的著作和文章，是 IPCC 第五次评估报告第三工作组共同主席。

Carolina Vera

Carolina Vera，阿根廷大气和海洋研究中心主任，该中心由布宜诺斯艾利斯大学、阿根廷国家科学理事会和法国国家科学研究中心联合成立。她也是布宜诺斯艾利斯大学精确与自然科学学院的全职教授。她于1992年在布宜诺斯艾利斯大学获大气科学博士学位，主要研究理解和预测南美地区气候变化。她是美国全球变化研究所科学咨询委员会委员，世界气候研究计划（WCRP）科学委员会成员，美国气象学会南半球气象与海洋学委员会主席。Vera博士在为不同经济领域的利益相关者（如农业、水、健康）开发气候信息工具方面拥有丰富的项目研究经验，是IPCC风险促进气候变化适应特别报告（SREX）主要作者。

Tetsuzo Yasunari

Tetsuzo Yasunari，东京人文和自然研究所教授、所长。他在东京大学获气象学博士学位，研究兴趣包括季风及热带气象和气候学，并扩展到气候与植被的相互影响、季风气候对人类活动的影响，以及跨学科亚洲气候研究。曾任东京大学东南亚研究中心助理教授（1977—1982）、筑波大学地球科学研究所副教授及教授（1982—2002），以及名古屋大学水圈大气研究中心教授（2002—2012）。还曾兼任日本海洋科学与技术中心全球环境变化前沿研究系统水文循环研究项目主任，1996—2002年期间任世界天气计划全球能量和水循环交换（WCRPGEWEX）亚洲季风实验组成员。后担任GEWEX SSG副主席以及WCRP联合科学委员会委员。他是IPCC第五次评估报告第一工作组编审。担任日本科学委员会委员，日本IGBP、WCRP和DIVERSITAS联合国家委员会主席。发表论文（著）约200篇（部）。

未来地球计划参与委员会委员

Future Earth Engagement Committee members

未来地球计划参与委员会由以下15位专家组成。

Jairam Ramesh，主席

Jairam Ramesh，印度国会议员，曾任经济和发展政策领域主管、部长，有30余年政务工作经验。2011—2012年间任联合国秘书长高级别全球可持续发展小组成员，在哥本哈根(2009)和坎昆(2010)联合国气候变化大会发挥重要作用。他发表了许多关于经济发展、能源、环境、全球化和印一中关系的著作。曾担任印度农村发展部部长、环境和森林部部长、商业与能源部部长，目前仍经常就与环境有关的问题发表评论。近期入选哈佛大学肯尼迪政治学院Fisher Family Fellow。他拥有工程和公共管理多个学位，曾就读于印度理工学院、卡内基·梅隆大学和麻省理工学院。其第三本著作《生态、增长和印度民主》2015年由牛津大学出版社出版。

James Fahn

James Fahn，“地球新闻网络”执行董事，该网络由全球5000余名关注环境问题的记者组成。作为一位主要关注发展中国家环境问题的新闻工作者，James还在加州大学伯克利分校研究生院担任客座教授。他的大部分职业生涯在泰国度过，曾担任英文日报The Nation的记者和编辑，还曾主持过具有泰国特色的电视节目。2003年他出版了《火上之地》，讲述了他在工作中发现的与东南亚环境有关问题和丑闻。此外，他还为《纽约时报》、《新闻周刊》、《经济学家》、《旧金山纪事报》、《雅加达邮报》、SciDev.net，Nature.com，《赫芬顿邮报》和《哥伦比亚新闻评论》撰稿。他负责“地球新闻网络”缅甸项目多年，是泰国环境记者学会的共同创始人，并曾担任福特基金会环境与发展项目助理。James曾因在The Nation上的环境报道获得联合国环境规划署颁发的Global 500 Award。

Vore Gana Seck

Vore Gana Seck，塞内加尔环保和可持续发展活动家，有25年的农村地区工作经验。她曾负责了多个关于荒漠化、粮食安全和地方发展项目和计划。作为绿色塞内加尔2000项目的创立者和项目主任，她在2005—2008年期间担任支持不发达国家发展理事会和西部非洲和中部非洲非政府组织论坛主席。1996—1999年间，她主持总部设在塞内加尔的国际非政府组织再生农业资源中心。她研究领域包括高度受气候变化影响的区域盐渍土的恢复，曾获得包括联合国开发署，Yves Rocher自然基金以及美国国会等颁发的多项国际国内奖项。哥本哈根气候峰会后，她向塞内加尔政府提议修订有关环境条款以融入气候变化问题。她曾在美国亚利桑那州立大学学习，专攻植物区系调查和自然资源管理地理信息系统（GIS）和土地退化评估。她还曾在比利时鲁汶天主教大学学习农学和生物学，在英国格拉斯哥大学研究气候变化法案，获得硕士学位。

Marina Grossi

Marina Grossi，巴西经济学家，2010年至今担任巴西企业可持续发展理事会（CEBDS）主席。自2005年在该理事会工作期间，她曾担任过执行董事、能源气候变化可持续发展建设与可持续金融工作组的协调员。Marina在政府领域工作经验丰富，1997—2001年期间曾作为巴西的谈判代表参加联合国气候变化大会。她还曾在巴西科技部负责过宣传工作，在巴西教育电视台负责过国际交流，在巴西旅游部担任过区域主任。2001—2003年期间，担任巴西论坛气候论坛协调人，并在2003年创办并主持一个可持续发展咨询公司，为政府和企业提供咨询；启动了“Carbon Disclosure Project”项目。通过这个项目，她加入CEBDS，开始关注企业的可持续发展。目前她是西班牙、巴西等多个国家和地区可持续发展理事会或顾问委员会的成员。

Masayo Hasegawa

Masayo Hasegawa，丰田汽车公司环境事务部项目总经理，日本经济团体联合会气候环境策略组世界可持续发展工商理事会（WBCSD）工作组代理主席，日本汽车制造商协会环境委员会气候变化分委会成员。她还是日本环境部中央环境理事会全球环境和环境政策委员会委员。她曾在美国运通国际股份有限公司和木原纪念横滨基金会生命科学部工作。1986年加入了笹川和平基金会（SPF），担任项目官员，负责环境问题12年。1992年她作为日本WBCSD联络官参与了在里约峰会提交“转变方向”议案。1997—2000年她曾担任庆应义塾大学环境与发展项目主任。她在日本关西学院大学获得社会学学士学位，美国塔夫茨大学获得国际关系MA。

Mario Hernandez

Mario Hernandez，国际摄影与遥感学会（ISPRS）拉美地区代表。他拥有数学背景，专攻应用卫星遥感技术。曾在IBM墨西哥和巴黎科学中心工作，后加入联合国环境计划署，协助发展中国家利用空间技术评估环境。他曾与联合国教科文组织建立了空间合作伙伴网络，工作包括帮助发展中国家描述发展对环境的影响；促进技术人员、科学家、决策者、教师和学生参与跨学科交流；利用空间数据得出易于理解信息提供给决策者；加强发展中国家理解和利用空间技术优势，监测、管理和维护资源的能力建设。他多次受邀为国际科学或决策类会议撰稿。

Yolanda Kakabadse

Yolanda Kakabadse，世界自然基金会国际主席（WWF）（2010年—）、厄瓜多尔前环境部长（1998年8月—2000年1月）。她曾在基多天主教大学攻读教育心理学。她的环境保护职业生涯开始于1979年，当时她被任命为设在基多的WWF执行董事，工作至1990年。在此期间，她促使WWF发展成为拉美地区最重要的环保组织之一。1993年她创建了拉丁美洲未来基金会，致力于促进拉丁美洲通过预防和处理冲突以达到可持续发展，她本人任该组织执行总裁，直至2006年，目前仍担任顾问委员会主席。

Amy Luers

Amy Luers，“斯科尔应对全球威胁基金会”气候主任，负责气候和水项目。她曾在谷歌担任高级项目经理，共同领导了一系列与气候风险管理有关的信息和通信技术项目。她还曾协同创办过一个拉美水资源管理NGO。主要研究脆弱性和恢复力，气候变化的影响和适应，以及气候政策。2013年，Luers入选首批 Bellagio/Poptech 大数据和系统恢复力会研究员。她是美国国家研究理事会地理地理科学委员会委员，是美国家气候评估持续评估报告的主要作者。Amy Luers 拥有斯坦福大学环境科学博士学位和国际政策研究硕士学位。

Tim Payn

Tim Payn，新西兰林业研究所首席科学家，负责经济、生态和气候研究小组。他的研究重点是可持续森林管理。他广泛参与国际和国内的可持续森林管理标准和指标的开发和应用，自 2003 年以来一直担任 12 国蒙特利尔进程技术咨询委员会的召集人。在新西兰国内，他发展并领导了可持续森林管理项目，项目涉及可持续森林管理环境、社会、经济以及文化方多个方面。他的研究兴趣在于如何通过科学—社会各领域—政府之间的相互作用实现科学的影响，是新西兰联合森林业主协会/农林业资源与环境委员会委员、新西兰气候变化中心治理小组成员，第一产业部研究创新和技术转让工作组成员。2014 年当选为新西兰林业研究所会员。他还担任国际林业研究组织联盟（IUFRO）可持续森林管理标准和指标工作组副协调员，推动了在森林、气候变化和人工林领域的国际科学合作。

Kari Raivio

Kari Raivio，围产医学教授，赫尔辛基大学初生婴儿重症室前主任。1994—1996 年期间担任该校医学院系主任，后任院长（至 2003 年），任赫尔辛基大学校长直至 2008 年退休。他的主要研究领域是新生儿健康。他是芬兰科学与人文院院和欧洲研究型大学联盟前任主席。他还曾担任国际科联科学计划和评估委员会副主席（2008—2011），是愿景规划工作组成员。该工作组的工作最终促成了未来地球计划诞生。他也是国际科学理事会未来国际研究合作前沿工作组成员。受芬兰首相办公室委托，Kari Raivio 曾评审国内外科学—政策咨询建议体系，并制定科学与政策对接的计划。作为 John Nurminen 基金会董事会员，他一直致力于降低磷酸盐注入波罗的海，造成藻类繁殖问题的研究。

Debra Roberts

Debra Roberts，南非德班 eThekwini Municipality 市环境规划和气候保护

部创立者和负责人。她是 IPCC 第五次评估报告第二工作组第 8 章(城市地区)和第 12 章(非洲)的主要作者。她是南非气候谈判小组的成员,在多个城市气候变化问题国际咨询机构任职(如洛克菲勒基金会亚洲城市气候变化恢复力网)。担任联合国人居署 HS—NET 咨询委员会副主席,负责指导 2011 年"城市与气候变化"的全球报告,是可持续发展和繁荣联盟的创始成员。她也是可持续发展解决方案网络专题组关于可持续城市的成员之一,参与制定 2015 后城市可持续发展目标。在城市开放空间规划、环境管理和城市气候保护等领域著述丰富,作品多次获奖。

Björn Stigson

Björn Stigson,哥德堡大学商业、经济及法律学院客座教授,担任国际应用系统分析研究所和瑞典皇家工程院高级顾问,本人开办咨询公司并任主席。Stigson 拥有丰富的国际商务经验。1995—2011 年期间,他任 WBCSD 主席。他还在包括美国国会、中国政府和德国政府等在内的多家国际公司、国际组织和多个政府的咨询委员会任职,是德国可持续发展政策同行评议主席。他是哈佛大学肯尼迪学院院长理事会成员之一。他任职的理事会和咨询机构还包括:摩纳哥基金会、西门子可持续发展咨询委员会、隆德大学国际工业环境经济研究所,加泰罗尼亚区长可持续发展顾问委员会、斯德哥尔摩经济学院可持续市场中心理事会。

Farooq Ullah

Farooq Ullah,2012 年 9 月起任利益相关者论坛执行主任。此前,他曾在英国可持续发展委员会工作 5 年。Farooq 的工作包括公共政策分析以及可持续发展战略、管理和决策。他的工作重点在政策咨询和宣传,以及利益相关者参与和能力建设。Farooq 有 9 年在国内和国际公共政策和可持续发展方面的工作经验,目前是英国议会环境审查委员会顾问。他也是总部设在伦敦的气候变化工作组"光明的未来"的创始成员之一。Farooq 拥有阿尔伯塔大学管理科学学士学位以及伦敦经济学院公共政策与管理硕士学位。

Scott Vaughan

Scott Vaughan，2013 年 4 月起任国际可持续发展研究所所长。此前，他曾连续五年担任加拿大联邦环境和可持续发展专员，也曾任美洲国家组织可持续发展部主任，卡内基国际和平基金会访问学者，北美自由贸易协定环境委员会主席，以及联合国环境计划署（UNEP）顾问。他曾在 UNEP 担任多个职位，1980 年代后期在皇家银行金融集团总部工作。他在蒙特爱立森大学获本科学位，在爱丁堡大学、达尔豪斯大学和伦敦政治经济学院获硕士学位。

Ruth Wolstenholme

Ruth Wolstenholme，苏格兰 Sniffer 公司总经理。Sniffer 公司是一个致力于传播可持续发展、环境管理和气候恢复力知识的慈善组织。她曾学习自然科学和社会科学，在多个环境保护和咨询机构工作。从学术研究项目、国家计划到以适应气候变化为出发点的合作计划，她经常与气候利益相关者与从业者合作交流，也在地方环境相关问题上直接与社区机构何团体合作，帮助他们发出自己的呼声，协同制定远景和行动计划。在她的领导下，Sniffer 公司在发展和完善苏格兰气候恢复日程中起到重要作用，包括发起并广为宣传“气候适应苏格兰计划”，该计划动员区域、国家和国际层面的力量参与能力建设，建立一个强大的行动网络。

未来地球计划执行主任

Future Earth Executive Director

Paul Shrivastava

Paul Shrivastava，2015 年 2 月被任命为未来地球计划执行主任。此前是加拿大康考迪亚大学 David O'Brien 可持续发展企业杰出教授并担任可持续发展企业中心主任。Shrivastava 在管理教育、创业、大型跨国公司咨询领域有 30 多年从业经验。他曾任纽约大学斯特恩商学院管理副教授、巴克内尔大学 Howard I. Scott 教授，帮助设立了法国 Nancy 商学院艺术和可持续企业国际研究主任之职。他是印度最大电脑公司之一 Hindustan 计算机有限公司管理团队成员，曾组建了一家非营利组织，顺利化解了 20 世纪 80 年代联合碳化物公司与印度政府之间博帕尔泄漏事故危机。他已经出版了 18 部著作，发表论文 100 余篇。

附录2 核心项目转化进程表

Appendix 2 Status of Core Project Transitions

未来地球计划将整合全球环境变化计划(GEC,包括DIVERSITAS、IGBP、IHDP、WCRP和ESSP)并在更宽泛的领域提出新倡议。原GEC项目将逐步转化为未来地球计划核心项目,程序为(1)项目科学指导委员会提交转化申请;(2)未来地球计划科学委会审议;(3)一旦评审通过,相关方签署备忘录(MoU),标志着该项目正式转化为未来地球核心项目。截至2015年3月31日,21个GEC项目已参与这一工作,其中5个项目已正式成为未来地球计划核心项目,其余16个的转化工作正在准备中。

核心项目转化进程

Status of Core Project Transitions

（Updated 31/03/2015）

（截至 2015 年 3 月 31 日）

序号	Core Project 核心项目	Programme 原 GEC 项目	Transition status 转化进程
1	ecoHEALTH 生态健康项目	DIVERSITAS 国际生物多样性计划	MoU signed MoU 已签
2	PECS Programme for Ecosystem Change and Society 生态系统变化和社会项目	ICSU 国际科学理事会	MoU signed MoU 已签
3	GLP Global Land Project 全球陆地项目	IGBP/IHDP 国际地圈生物圈计划/国际全球环境变化人文因素计划	MoU signed MoU 已签
4	LOICZ Land-Ocean Interactions in the Coastal Zone 海岸带陆海相互作用计划	IGBP/IHDP 国际地圈生物圈计划/国际全球环境变化人文因素计划	MoU being signed MoU 签署中
5	IRG Integrated Risk Governance 综合风险防范项目	IHDP 国际全球环境变化人文因素计划	MoU being signed MoU 签署中
6	UGEC Urbanization and Global Environmental Change 城镇化和全球环境变化项目	IHDP 国际全球环境变化人文因素计划 Revised statement received	收到转化声明修改稿
7	ecoSERVICES 生态服务项目	DIVERSITAS 国际生物多样性计划	Revised statement received 收到转化声明修改稿

续表

序号	Core Project 核心项目	Programme 原 GEC 项目	Transition status 转化进程
8	bioDISCOVERY 生态发现项目	DIVERSITAS 国际生物多样性计划	Reviews provided to Project 评审意见返回项目
9	bioGENESIS 生物合成项目	DIVERSITAS 国际生物多样性计划	Reviews provided to Project 评审意见返回项目
10	PAGES Past Global Change 过去全球变化	IGBP 国际地圈生物圈计划	Reviews provided to Project 评审意见返回项目
11	SOLAS Surface Ocean-Lower Atmosphere Study 浅层海洋与低层大气研究	IGBP/WCRP 国际地圈生物圈计划/世界气候变化	Statement under review 评审中
12	MAIRS Monsoon Asia Integrated Regional Study 季风亚洲区域集成研究项目	ESSP 地球系统科学联盟	Statement under review 评审中
13	ESG Earth System Governance 地球系统管理项目	IHDP 国际全球环境变化人文因素计划	Statement under review 评审中
14	IHOPE Integrated History and Future of People on Earth 人类历史与未来的整合项目	IHDP 国际全球环境变化人文因素计划	Statement under review 评审中
15	GWSP Global Water System Project 全球水系统计划	ESSP 地球系统科学联盟	Statement under review 评审中
16	GMBA Global Mountain Biodiversity Assessment 全球山地生物多样性评估计划	DIVERSITAS 国际生物多样性计划	in development 转化准备进行中

续表

序号	Core Project 核心项目	Programme 原 GEC 项目	Transition status 转化进程
17	IMBER Integrated Marine Biogeochemistry and Ecosystem Research 海洋生物地球化学和生态系统的整合研究项目	IGBP 国际地圈生物圈计划	In development 转化准备进行中
18	AIMES Analysis, Integration and Modelling of the Earth System 地球科学计划地球系统分析、综合与模拟科学计划	IGBP 国际地圈生物圈计划	In development 转化准备进行中
19	iLEAPS Integrated Land Ecosystem-Atmosphere Processes Study 陆地生态系统与大气过程综合研究计划	IGBP 国际地圈生物圈计划	In development 转化准备进行中
20	IGAC International Global Atmospheric Chemistry 国际全球大气化学计划	IGBP 国际地圈生物圈计划	In development 转化准备进行中
21	GCP Global Carbon Project 全球碳计划	ESSP 地球系统科学联盟	In development 转化准备进行中

附录3　未来地球计划中国国家委员会简介

Appendix 3　A Brief Introduction to the Chinese National Committee for Future Earth

未来地球计划中国国家委员会(以下简称CNC-FE)于2014年3月21日在北京成立。CNC-FE由中国科学技术协会、中国科学院、中国工程院、中国社会科学院和国家自然科学基金委员会联合支持，旨在组织协调中国科学家参与未来地球计划，积极利用国际资源促进我国生态文明建设。CNC-FE的成立标志着中国正式、全面地参与国际未来地球计划。

结合未来地球计划主题和国家科技发展需求，CNC-FE确定了14个重点研究领域，并成立了相应的工作组。通过实施项目、召开国际、国内会议、推广宣传等一系列的活动为推动未来地球计划在中国的实施发挥了重要作用。

CNC-FE确立了以下14个重点领域：

(1)环境污染及健康

(2)城镇化与社会和谐发展

(3)季风区气候变异与人类动

(4)全球变化及关键区响应

(5)食品、能源供给与未来发展

(6)生物多样性与生态系统服务

(7)产业转型与绿色生产

(8)变化环境下的灾害预警

(9)东亚传统文化与可持续性发展

(10)极区可持续性发展

(11)地球系统观测和知识服务

(12)地球系统模式、气候经济模式与气候变化科学决策

(13)海洋与海岸带可持续发展

(14)青藏高原及其全球气候变化

CNC-FE 构成

未来地球计划中国国家委员会由来自自然科学、工程和社会科学等各领域的40余名专家组成，充分体现了学科交叉、科学为社会服务的理念。委员会由中国科学技术协会副主席、中国科学院院士、未来地球计划科学委员会委员秦大河担任主席，中国科学技术协会副主席、书记处书记张勤研究员、中国工程院杜祥琬院士、中国科学院生态环境研究中心傅伯杰院士、国家自然科学基金委员会副主任刘丛强院士、中国社会科学院城市发展与环境研究所所长潘家华研究员、中国科学院大气物理研究所吴国雄院士任副主席。CNC-FE秘书处设在中国科学院大气物理研究所大气科学和地球流体力学数值模拟国家重点实验室，周天军研究员任秘书长。为在更高层面指导委员会的工作，还成立了由全国政协副主席、中国科学技术协会主席、中国科学院院士韩启德担任主席的指导委员会。

CNC-FE 指导委员会

主　席

韩启德　全国政协副主席、中国科学技术协会主席、中国科学院院士（心血管病理生理、分子药理）

委　员

周　济　中国工程院院长、中国工程院院士（机械制造与自动化）

李静海　中国科学院副院长、中国科学院院士（化学工程）

李　扬　中国社会科学院副院长（经济学）

徐冠华　中国科学院院士（林业、遥感）

孙鸿烈　中国科学院院士（土壤地理与土地资源）

陈宜瑜　中国科学院院士（鱼类学、动物分类学）

未来地球计划中国国家委员会委员

主　席

秦大河　中国科学技术协会副主席、中国科学院院士（冰冻圈与全球变化）

副主席（按姓氏笔画排序）

刘丛强　国家自然科学基金委员会副主任、中国科学院院士（地球化学）

杜祥琬　中国工程院院士（应用物理与能源发展）

吴国雄　中国科学院大气物理研究所研究员、中国科学院院士（大气动力学与气候动力学）

张　勤　中国科学技术协会副主席、书记处书记（核反应堆）

傅伯杰　中国科学院生态环境研究中心研究员、中国科学院院士（自然地理与景观生态学）

潘家华　中国社会科学院城市发展与环境研究所所长（城市发展与环境）

委　员（按姓氏笔画排序）

丁一汇　中国气象局气候变化特别顾问、中国工程院院士（天气与气候学）

丁永建　中国科学院寒区旱区环境与工程研究所研究员（冰冻圈与水循环）

于宏源　上海国际问题研究院比较政治和公共政策研究所所长（地缘政治）

马克平　中国科学院植物研究所研究员（生物多样性与生物安全）

王　浩　中国水利水电科学研究院水资源研究所所长、中国工程院院士（流域水循环、生态环境效应）

王　镭　中国社会科学院国际合作局局长（贸易投资）

毛其智　清华大学建筑学院副院长、国际欧亚科学院院士（城市与区域规划设计）

申倚敏　中国科学院学部工作局生命地学办公室主任（公共管理）

史培军　北京师范大学常务副校长（自然地理学、资源开发与减灾）

吕永龙　中国科学院生态环境研究中心副主任（生态学、环境管理与政策）

朱　彤　北京大学环境科学与工程学院院长（大气化学、环境与健康）

朱永官　中国科学院城市环境研究所所长（土壤生物学）

伍业钢　东方园林股份有限公司生态城市规划院院长（生态系统复杂性、全球变化生态学）

刘　健　中国科学院地理科学与资源研究所研究员（生态系统管理与适应）

刘卫东　中国科学院地理科学与资源研究所所长助理（中国区域发展、经济地理学）

安芷生　中国科学院地球环境研究所研究员、中国科学院院士（第四纪地质、过去全球变化）

严晋跃　瑞典皇家理工学院和梅拉达伦大学教授，未来能源中心主任；国际应用能源创新研究院院长（能源及环境工程）

杜德斌　华东师范大学资源与环境科学学院城市与区域经济系主任教育部战略研究基地主任（科技政策与区域创新、世界经济地理）

何建坤　清华大学能源环境经济研究所所长（能源系统工程与应对气候变化）

张人禾　中国气象科学研究院研究员（热带大尺度海气相互作用、亚洲季风研究）

张小曳　中国气象科学研究院研究员（大气气溶胶）

张开逊　北京机械工业自动化研究所研究员（电子物理与传感技术）

张永生　国务院发展研究中心发展战略和区域经济研究部副部长（发展经济学）

张宇燕　中国社会科学院世界政治与经济研究所所长（宏观经济）

张建生　中国科学技术协会国际联络部部长（管理学）

张海滨　北京大学国际关系学院国际政治系副系主任（国际环境政治、中国环境外交和联合国研究）

陈　军　国家基础地理信息中心总工程师（地理信息系统）

陈　曦　中国科学院新疆生态与地理研究所所长（干旱区水文学与水资源）

陈大可　国家海洋局第二海洋研究所卫星海洋环境动力学国家重点实验室主任（物理海洋学）

陈德亮　瑞典哥德堡大学教授、瑞典皇家科学院院士（区域气候学与气候动力学）

赵白鸽　中国红十字会党组书记、常务副会长（人口科学、生物医学）

饶平凡　浙江工商大学食品与生物工程学院教授（食品工程）

姚檀栋　中国科学院青藏高原研究所研究员中国科学院院士（冰川环境与全球变化）

骆华松　云南师范大学旅游与地理科学学院院长（人文地理）

顾朝林　清华大学建筑学院城市规划系教授（城市与区域规划、城市地理学）

倪四义　新华社总编室副主任

郭华东　中国科学院遥感与数字地球研究所所长、中国科学院院士（遥感科学与应用）

效存德　中国科学院寒区旱区环境与工程研究所研究员（自然地理）

陶　澍　北京大学城市与环境学院院长、中国科学院院士（区域尺度环境过程）

崔　鹏　中国科学院水利部成都山地灾害与环境研究所研究员、中国科学院院士（山地灾害与水土保持）

符淙斌　南京大学气候与全球变化研究院院长、中国科学院院士（气候和全球变化）

葛全胜　中国科学院地理科学与资源研究所所长（全球变化）

葛剑雄　上海复旦大学图书馆馆长教育部社会科学委员会委员（历史学、历史地理）

董文杰　北京师范大学地表过程与资源生态国家重点实验室副主任（气候动力学、气候理论与预测和全球变化）

秘书处

周天军（秘书长）　中国科学院大气物理研究所（气候动力学、气候模拟）

林　征　中国科学院大气物理研究所

金　楠　中国科学院大气物理研究所

王传艺　中国科学院大气物理研究所

艾丽坤　中国科学院大气物理研究所

黄　磊　国家气候中心

王伟财　中国科学院青藏高原研究所

张　莹　中国社会科学院城市发展与环境研究所

秦久怡　中国科学技术协会国际科技会议中心

吴波龙　中国社会科学院国际合作局国际组织处

袁　越　中国科学技术协会国际科技会议中心

陈　蕾　中国科学技术协会国际联络部国际组织处

庄　岩　中国科学院国际合作局国际组织处

陈康君　中国科学院大气物理研究所

关于 CNC-FE 的更多信息请见 CNC-FE 网站：

http://cnc-fe.cast.org.cn/index.html